The Great American Je
Second Edit

Ron Kizer & Amanda Stock

For more information:
BestJerkyRecipes.com

Photography & Cover Image by:
Amanda Stock Photography

ISBN-13: 978-1494984663
ISBN-10: 1494984660

Copyright © 2013 Amanda Stock. All rights Reserved. No part of this book may be used or reproduced in any manner without written permission, except in the case of brief quotations in articles, interviews or reviews.

Limit of Liability and Disclaimer of Warranty: The author makes no representations or warranties with respect to the accuracy or completeness of this work and specifically disclaim all warranties. The advice and strategies contained here may not be suitable for every situation. The author is not liable in any way for damages arising from the information provided. All links are for informational purposes only and are not warranted for content, accuracy or any other purpose. The author does not endorse any information the organization or websites listed may provide.

Dedicated to Dad.

Foreword

We grew up helping make (and mostly stealing samples of) our Dad's delicious beef jerky. Sometimes he would let us pick flowers from the backyard and put them in our dehydrator and other times he would turn an eye while we snuck in it to steal a piece of warm, delicious jerky that had yet to pass the dryness test. As a hobby, our Dad collected hundreds of jerky marinade recipes over the years. He complied all of his favorite recipes into a homemade cookbook, stapled it together and called it The Great American Beef Jerky Cookbook. He shared this book with family and friends.

Seventeen years after our Dad created the first version of The Great America Beef Jerky Cookbook, we found a copy and decided to test out a recipe. We used our oven and made "Good Ol' Fashion" jerky. It was even more delicious than we remembered! We shared the jerky with friends and they loved it. We started making and sharing a lot of jerky and decided the best way to share was to update the cookbook and publish the recipes.

A cowboy at heart, our Dad believed that homemade jerky was one of the finer things in life. He had only one rule for jerky making: *Save some for others.*

And so, to honor our Dad's cardinal rule of jerky makin', we've publish this book of recipes to share with you, in hopes that you will enjoy one of the finer things in life - homemade jerky.

Enjoy!

Sincerely,
Amanda

Table of Contents

Foreword 3

Table of Contents 4

Introduction 8

Important Warnings 10

History of Jerky 11

Drying Equipment & Instructions 12

Ovens 13

Smokers 16

Dehydrators 17

Which Meats to Use 19

Pork 19

Beef 19

Lamb 20

Poultry 20

Game Meats 20

Ground Meats 21

Meat Preparation 22

Drying Jerky 28

Testing for Dryness 29

Storage of Jerky 30

Allergy & Special Diet Considerations 31

    Wheat & Gluten 31

    Paleo Diet, Soy 31

    Diabetic, Sugar Free 32

    Other 32

    Soy Free Sauce 33

    Special Diet Worcestershire Sauce 33

    Reduced Sugar Brown Sugar 33

The Jerky Marinade Recipes 35

    Basic Beef Jerky 36

    Just Plain Great Jerky 36

    Good Ol'Fashion Jerky 37

    Full Flavoured Jerky 37

    Pepper Hot Jerky 38

    Backpackers Delight 38

    Cowboy Jerky 39

    Old West Jerky 39

    Barbecue Jerky 40

    Hot & Spicy Jerky 40

    Sweet & Sour Jerky 41

    Fiesta Jerky 41

    Oriental Jerky 42

    Ragin' Cajun Jerky 42

Peppered Teriyaki Jerky 43

Teriyaki Jerky 43

Bottle of Soy Jerky 44

Mild Mexican Jerky 44

Granny's Jerky 45

Home Style Jerky 45

Hawaiian Jerky 46

EZ Jerky 46

Yankee Jerky 47

Baja Jerky 47

Oriental Jerky 48

Taj Mahal Jerky 48

Colorado Jerky 49

Valley Jerky 49

Jerky Time 50

West Coast Jerky 50

East Coast Jerky 51

Dixie Jerky 51

Seven Stuff Jerky 52

Hot & Tangy Jerky 52

Dale's Cheap Jerky 53

Frontier Jerky 53

Damn Good Jerky 54

New England Jerky 54

Old Basic Jerky 55

T-Beef Jerky 55

Well-Seasoned Jerky 56

Peppered Jerky 56

Alabama Honey Jerky 57

Slow & Sweet Jerky 57

Herb Jerky 58

Smoke & Spice Jerky 58

Thai Beef Jerky 59

Alabama Backwoods Jerky 59

Southern Cured Jerky 60

Onion Beef Jerky 60

Jesse James Jerky 61

Post Script 62

Bibliography 63

Introduction

Homemade jerky is easy to make and tastes delicious. It is a mess free, nutritious snack that is easy to take on the go. Jerky is perfect for road trips and camping, but also great for movies, sharing as a gift or as an afternoon snack. It can be made in bulk and stores easily.

The equipment required to make jerky is minimal and you most likely have all the tools you need in your kitchen already. With the exception of pork, you can make jerky from almost any kind of meat, including beef, turkey, salmon and game meats.

Unlike other Jerky books, each marinade recipe is formulated for use with one pound of meat. This makes it easy for the jerky making hobbyist to try a variety of recipes or make small batches. If you plan to use more meat, simply multiply the recipe to suit the amount of meat you are going to use.

Using the recipes in this book, it is unlikely that you will want to buy jerky in the store ever again!

Before you get started with the marinade recipes, be sure to read through the following pages for safety tips, equipment, directions and allergy considerations.

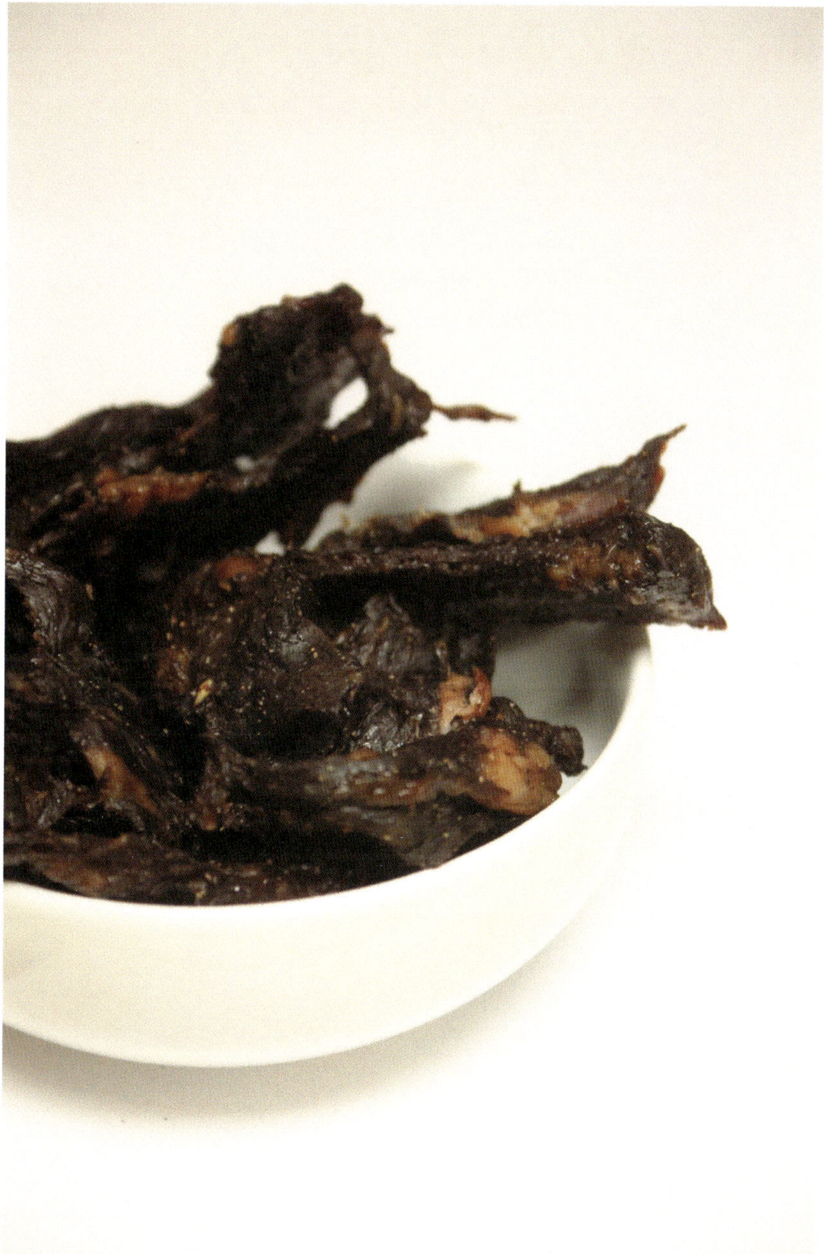

Important Warnings

- Do not use tainted meat.
- Do not use pork.
- Do not save or re-use marinades.
- Close supervision is required around children.
- Sharp knives are dangerous.
- Read all instructions before beginning.
- Do not touch hot cooking surfaces.

History of Jerky

The process of making jerky was created and used by Native Americans, as early as 1550. As settlers arrived in America, Native Americans shared the process with them. Native Americans called it "Charqui." Europeans, with their foreign accents, pronounced it "Jerky" and that pronunciation of the word stuck.

Jerky was the perfect food to have during a time when the availability of fresh food was not always certain. It grew to be very popular with cowboys and pioneers because it was a snack that was dense in nutrients and could be stored easily for long periods of time. The ability to hunt meat and make jerky was a valuable skill, since it provided a source of food that was easy to transport as the settlers moved west.

The recipes they used consisted of marinating meat with dried or fresh fruits, animal fats, herbs or spices. They would either lay the meat out in the sun to dry or they used fire to smoke it. They found they could use different types of wood in the smoking process and it would alter the taste and the flavor of the meat as it cooked.

Today, we have a wide variety of ingredients available to us to make excellent jerky marinades and it can be easily made in your home oven, dehydrator or smoker.

Drying Equipment & Instructions

Kitchen ovens, outdoor charcoal smokers, electric smokers and dehydrators are the best choices for making jerky at home. Due to safety concerns, air or sun drying methods are not recommended. Sun or air drying can be safely used for fruits, vegetables or flowers, however with meat, the potential for food position is not worth the risk.

The two main points to consider when selecting a drying method are temperature control and operating costs.

Oven drying may be more expensive than using a smoker, and an electric dehydrator may even be more expensive than using an oven or a smoker. However, using the kitchen oven is certainly more cost-effective than opting to purchase a special unit when only small amounts of jerky are being made.

Jerky making requires that the temperature remain constant throughout the drying process. Whichever device you use, should be able to maintain a temperature of 160 degrees for anywhere from 4-12 hours, depending on the thickness and cut of the meat.

The key to making jerky is simply to use good marinade sauces and cook the meat slowly. Allowing the meat to reach an internal temperature of 160 degrees will ensure any bacteria in the meat is killed.

Ovens

On some older overs, the lowest temperature setting is around 200 degrees. This is too hot for drying jerky. At that temperature the meat will begin to cook on the outside and not become dry on the inside. As long as it can be done safely, an older style oven can be adopted simply by propping the oven door open slightly.

Test your oven for about one hour before using it to dry any food by placing an oven thermometer on the top shelf towards the back. One hour should be adequate to determine the average temperature inside the oven.

Some ovens come with a warm setting, often noted on the temperature dial as WM. This setting typically produces temperatures between 120 and 180 degrees. Consult your oven manual to determine the exact temperature, as this may be a good option for making jerky.

Keep in mind you will need to main a constant temperature of around 160 degrees and you will need to be able to sustain that temperature over a long period of time. If you are unable to maintain 160 degrees over a long period of time, then your oven should not be used for drying meat.

Another important item to consider is the racks that will hold the meat strips of jerky while drying.

Since any item that dries becomes smaller in size, be sure that the racks that you intend to use will not allow small pieces to fall through. Typically meat will lose ¾ of its weight during the drying process. That equates to approximately ⅛ of its total volume.

Regular oven racks may not be suitable for drying jerky. The spacing of the rails on the racks may be too wide. If you find that the spacing on your oven racks is too wide, consider purchasing specific oven racks that are made for drying foods. These types of racks are available at your local cooking store or Amazon.com for less than $10 per rack.

Also available, are sets of stackable racks with a pan below to catch grease and marinade from falling on the bottom of your oven. For more information on the types of racks available, visit **BestJerkyRecipes.com** for reviews and options.

Alternatively, you can use aluminum foil to line the bottom of your oven to catch any drippings.

When drying meat in the oven, air circulation is important. Be sure that whatever you use for racks will allow adequate airflow around the meat. You should plan on having at least two inches between each rack and at least one inch around all four sides of the rack.

Placing the meat directly on baking sheets or aluminum foil will not work due to the small amount of grease that escapes from the meat as it dries. This would leave the meat lying in the grease during cooking and not allow for adequate air circulation.

Smokers

Smokers are a great way to make jerky. The outdoor units have the benefit of adding flavor with various types of wood, like mesquite or hickory, in addition to the use of marinade sauces.

Since the racks of an outdoor style smoker resemble those found in your kitchen oven, the same applies with regards to rack spacing and air circulation. The difference is that the racks are usually round instead of square. Just be sure that whatever you use for racks will allow adequate airflow around the meat. You should plan on having at least two inches between each rack and at least one inch around all four sides of the rack.

Like oven drying, the heat on the charcoal smokers is controlled by opening and closing various vents on the side and top of the unit. Most modern dehydrators and smokers are equipped with a built in temperature gauge. This gauge may only show a relative range, but with the some experimenting, you should be able to get a good idea for the approximate inside temperature.

Dehydrators

Electric dehydrators have been around for a long time and are still a favorite of among jerky makers. These units come in a variety of shapes and sizes. Some are expandable and some are not. The better models have a fan incorporated into their design to aid in circulating air.

Electric dehydrators are also equipped with thermostats to control the temperature and are therefore the simplest to use with its "set and forget" operation. They usually range from $35 to $300, but they're well worth the investment if you make a lot of jerky or intend on drying your own fruits, vegetables or flowers as well.

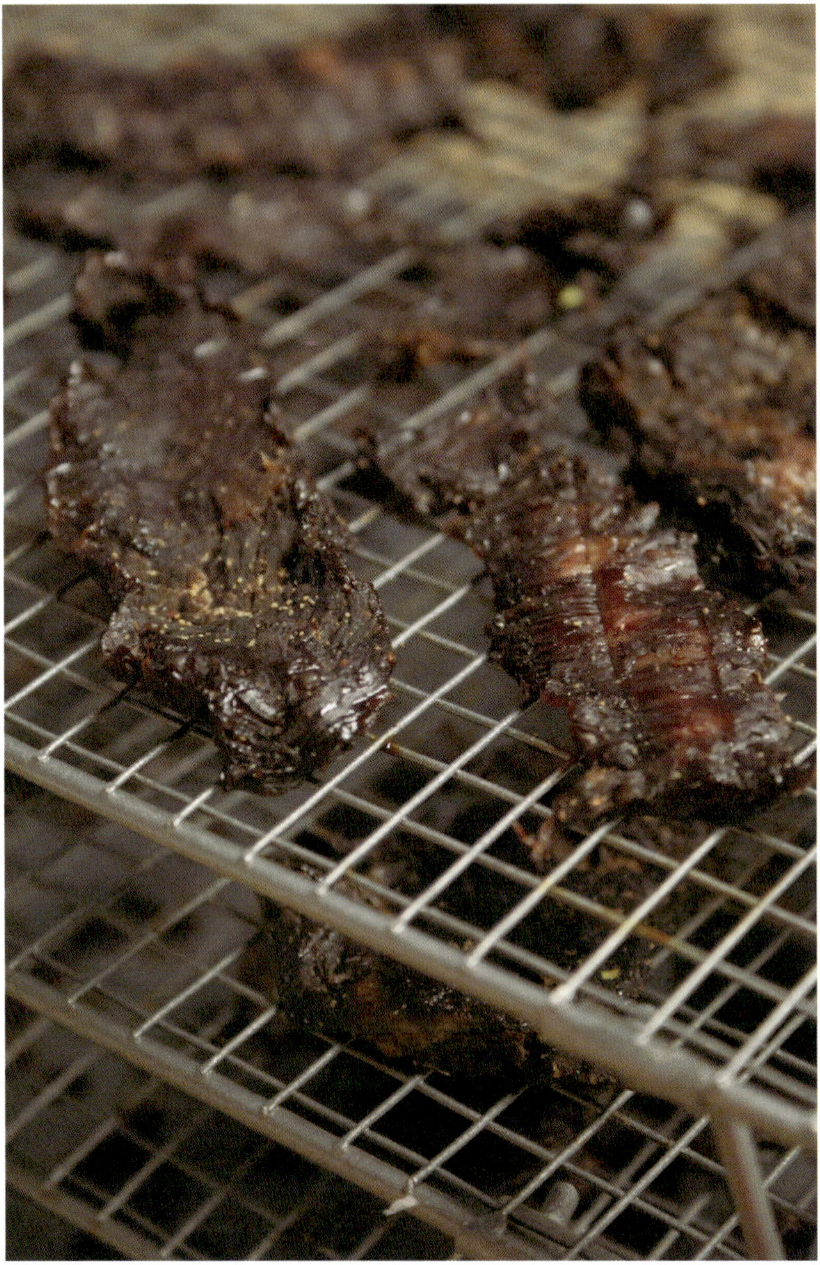

Which Meats to Use

Another choice you have in making your own jerky is which type of meat to use. Making this choice is where the fun begins. Different types of meat will yield different textures and tastes to the finished jerky.

Important Warning: When selecting a piece of meat, be sure that the meat is fresh. If there is any sign of tainting, do not use it for jerky.

Pork

Pork is not suitable for jerky making' because of the low cooking temperatures involved. At these low temperatures the bacteria, trichinella may not be killed. Trichinella can cause a fatal disease called Trichinosis. Do not use pork for jerky.

Beef

Beef is the most popular type of jerky because it is readily available in grocery stores. Lean meat contains less fat content. It is not necessary to purchase choice grade meats. Less expensive cuts often yield better jerky. Flank, Round, Steak and Sirloin Tip are usually less expensive per pound because of lack of fat and bone material. Rump cuts contain more gristle (cartilage, rough, inedible tissue in meat), but a few minutes of knife work causes rump cuts to become an excellent choice for making jerky.

Lamb

Lamb can be used to make jerky, although it isn't always the best choice due to the large amount of fat content. If you have the cutting skills to separate the muscle from fat, then the muscle can make great tasting jerky and the remaining fat can be used in cooking other foods, such as roasted potatoes.

Poultry

As a general rule, poultry is not practical for jerky making due to the amount of bone material. One exception is Turkey jerky. Turkey jerky is certainly worth trying. For other types of poultry, the meat could be ground and used for jerky.

Game Meats

Elk, Deer, Bear and Antelope make excellent jerky. As a precaution with any game meat, it is best to freeze the meat for at least thirty days prior to using it. Any cuts may be used.

Ground Meats

Ground meat gives a different texture to jerky than whole meat strips. Ground meat could be used as long as good meat preparation processes are used to ensure that the meat is not tainted and the tools are available to shape the meat into sticks or strips. There are generally three methods for shaping ground meat.

1.) Jerky guns are available which resemble a caulking gun. The marinated ground meat is loaded into the chamber and then squeezed out onto the racks.
2.) Ground meat can be frozen and then sliced into thin strips.
3.) Ground meat can be thoroughly mixed, flattened and then sliced into strips and placed onto the racks gently.

Meat Preparation

As you try out the recipes in this book, use a notebook or the margins to keep track of which marinade was used with which type of meat and what the outcome was. After some testing, you will begin to develop your own favorite combinations.

To use the recipes contained in this book, begin with one pound of lean meat per marinade recipe. If you plan to use more than one pound, multiply the recipe to suit your needs.

Place the meat into the freezer for about one hour to partially freeze the cut. This will make slicing thin strips easier.

When the meat is partially frozen, firm but not solid, slice it into ¼ inch thick strips. Try to keep the meat thin, since a thicker slice of meat will take a long time to dehydrate. In addition, a thicker slice of meat may not dry completely inside, while the outside may be overdone.

An electric meat knife works excellent for this purpose, but you can get along very well with just a good sharp knife.

Meat cut across the grain will be more tender than those cut along the grain. Meat cut along the grain tends to be chewier. This however is simply a matter of personal choice. Try both cuts.

The next step is to marinate the meat. Choose a container with a tight fitting lid or use plastic wrap and a rubber band to seal around a loose fitting lid.

Begin by coating the first layer of strips on both sides with the marinade mix. Place a layer of meat into a suitable sized container. Continue coating and layering the remaining pieces of meat.

Placement of the strips within the container is not important. In fact, it is a good idea to shake the container periodically during the marinade process to insure that the meat is fully coated.

When all of the meat is in the container, put the lid on tightly, and set the container into the refrigerator overnight.

After the meat has been in the marinade overnight, it is now ready to dry. When you are ready to dry the meat, begin by laying strips of meat onto the drying racks. Do not overlap any of the pieces. This will ensure good air circulation. You may want to place a piece of aluminum foil or baking sheet on the bottom of the oven or dehydrator to catch grease drippings.

Continue placing strips on until the rack is full or you have run out of meat. Change to another rack if the first gets full. Remember to allow for adequate air circulation, both between pieces of meat and throughout multiple racks.

Drying Jerky

Depending on the device you are using to dry your jerky and the thickness or cut of your meat, cooking times may vary. The key to getting great tasting jerky is to cook it slowly. However, the meat must reach an internal temperature of 160 degrees to ensure it is safe to eat.

Oven drying: Set the temperature on your oven so it maintains 160 degrees and let the meat cook 5 to 6 hours.

Smoker drying: Maintain 160 degrees and let the meat cook 5 to 6 hours.

Dehydrator drying: Set the temperature to 160 degrees and let the meat cook for 3 to 4 hours. Then the temperature may be reduced as low as 120 degrees for another 2 to 4 hours.

Testing for Dryness

One of the best tasting meats you will ever have will be a perfectly marinated, slow cooked, warm piece of jerky. As the drying process takes place, a certain amount of self-control will be required. It is true that the chef must "test" the product, but you will want to save some to share.

After a few hours of cooking, take out a sample piece and allow it to cool. Try to bend it in the middle. The piece should bend and crack but not break in half.

If your piece fails the dryness test, use it as a taste test or return it to cook a bit longer. Allow up to 2 additional hours of cook time if your sample piece fails the dryness test.

Many have a preference for tender jerky; the longer you dehydrate it the more brittle it becomes. When the test piece bends and cracks, but does not break, its finished.

Storage of Jerky

Allow the finished jerky to cool, and then, if required, use either scissors or a sharp knife to cut the pieces into 3-4 inch long sections. Jerky stores best in a cool, dry location.

Use "zip-lock" baggies or containers and store it in the refrigerator or in the freezer.

Jerky containing salt may be stored at room temperature for up to two months. Because you are relying on the salt to help preserve the meat, do not use reduced sodium soy sauce in your marinade mix. If storing at room temperature, avoid air tight containers for jerky.

Allergy & Special Diet Considerations

Wheat & Gluten

Many of the marinade recipes within this book contain soy sauce and Worcestershire sauce, both contain wheat. There are several brands which offer gluten free and wheat free versions of these sauces. These sauces are readily available on Amazon.com. You can visit **BestJerkyRecipes.com** for more information on gluten free and wheat free options.

Paleo Diet, Soy

Jerky is a great snack choice for a Paleo diet, however many of the recipes in the book make use of soy sauce, which is made from legumes, or Worcestershire sauce, which is made with added sugar or soy. If you are on the Paleo diet see the recipes on Page 32 for **Soy Free Sauce** and **Special Diet Worcestershire Sauce**.

Diabetic, Sugar Free

If the recipes call for a sugar, consider using a sugar substitute or admitting it from the recipe. Because molasses is sweet, yet low in sugar, consider using the **Reduced Sugar Brown Sugar** recipe on Page 32. You can also sprinkle a sugar substitute on the jerky when it is finished dehydrating.

Other

If other ingredients are not included in your diet, do not be afraid to experiment by replacing them or excluding them from your marinade recipe.

Soy Free Sauce

1 1/2 cups broth
4 tsp balsamic vinegar
1 tsp dark molasses
1/4 tsp ground ginger
1/4 tsp garlic powder
1/2 tsp sea salt
fresh ground pepper to taste

Special Diet Worcestershire Sauce

1/2 cup apple cider vinegar
2 Tablespoons water
2 Tablespoons coconut aminos
1/4 teaspoon ground ginger
1/4 teaspoon mustard powder
1/4 teaspoon onion powder
1/4 teaspoon garlic powder
1/8 teaspoon cinnamon
1/8 teaspoon ground pepper

Reduced Sugar Brown Sugar

(Equal to 1/4 cup brown sugar)
1/4 tablespoon molasses
1/4 cup sweetener

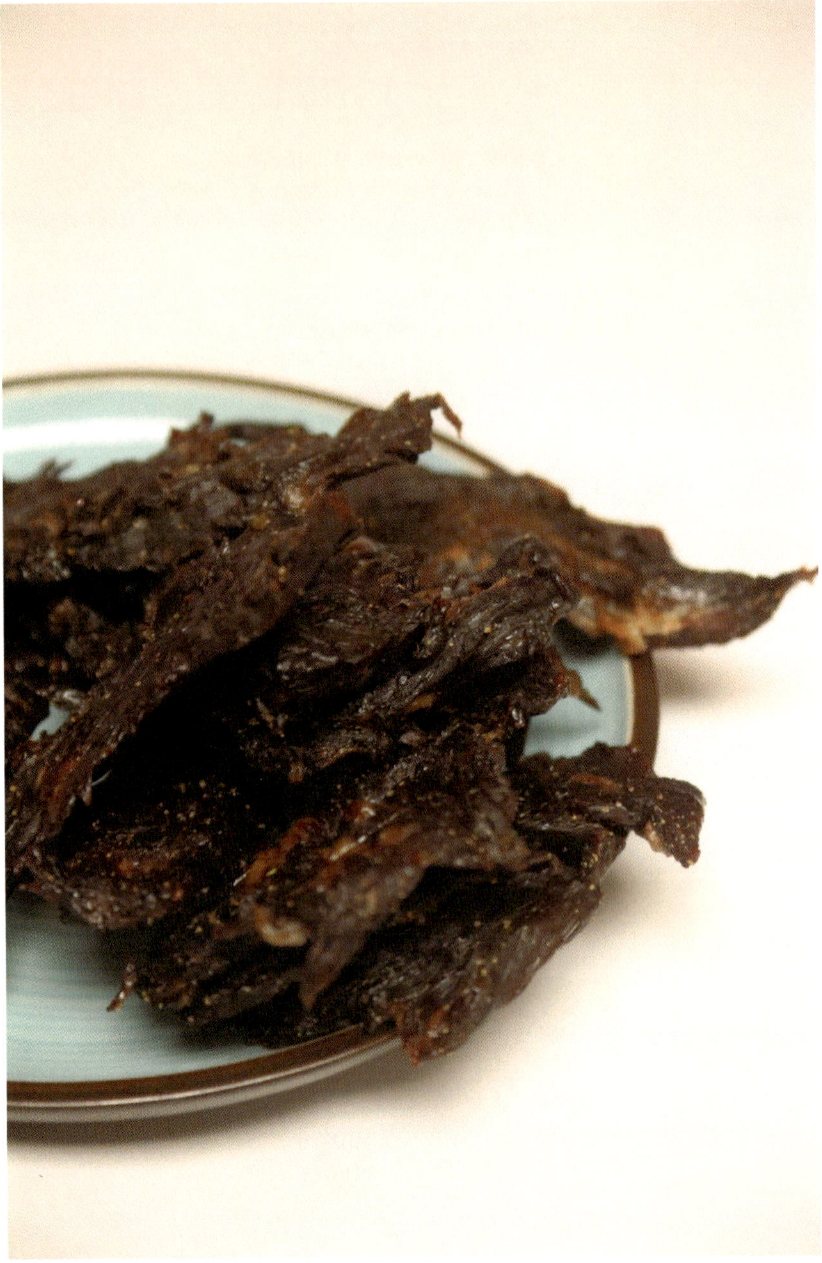

The Jerky Marinade Recipes

- All of the recipes in this book are for one pound of thinly sliced lean meat.

- Do not attempt to re-use any of these marinade sauces. Always start by making a new batch of marinade mix.

- Be sure to use the blank areas on each page to make your own notes, so you can start collecting your own favorite recipes.

Basic Beef Jerky

1 teaspoon soy sauce
4 teaspoons worcestershire sauce
1 teaspoon ketchup
¼ teaspoon garlic powder
¼ teaspoon onion salt
¼ teaspoon black pepper

Just Plain Great Jerky

1 tablespoon liquid smoke
1 package of Shilling Meat Marinade
(omit oil from Shilling's recipe)
1 teaspoon salt
¾ cup water

Good Ol'Fashion Jerky

¾ teaspoon salt
¼ teaspoon black pepper
1 tablespoon brown sugar
1 garlic clove (crushed)
1 tablespoon soy sauce
1 tablespoon worcestershire sauce

Full Flavoured Jerky

2 ½ tablespoon brown sugar
1 ½ tablespoon white or cane sugar
1 tablespoon ginger
1 garlic clove (crushed)
½ cup soy sauce
1 tablespoon tarragon

Pepper Hot Jerky

1 cup red wine vinegar
½ cup salad oil
⅓ cup brown sugar
⅛ cup Tabasco sauce
¼ teaspoon salt
¼ teaspoon marjoram
¼ teaspoon rosemary
¾ cup chopped onion
1 garlic clove (crushed)

Backpackers Delight

4 teaspoons salt
1 teaspoon black pepper
1 teaspoon chili powder
1 teaspoon garlic salt
1 teaspoon onion powder
¼ teaspoon cayenne pepper
3 "dashes" of liquid smoke
½ cup of water

Cowboy Jerky

1 teaspoon salt
⅓ teaspoon black pepper
⅛ teaspoon cinnamon
⅛ teaspoon ground cloves
⅛ teaspoon ground cumin
1 ½ teaspoon curry powder
½ teaspoon garlic powder
1 teaspoon ground ginger

Old West Jerky

1 teaspoon salt
1 ¼ teaspoon black pepper
1 teaspoon garlic powder
2 teaspoons Worcestershire sauce
2 tablespoons liquid smoke

Barbecue Jerky

1 teaspoon salt
1 ¼ teaspoon black pepper
¼ teaspoon cayenne powder
1 teaspoon onion powder
½ teaspoon dry mustard
3 tablespoons cinnamon
⅓ cup red wine vinegar
⅓ cup ketchup

Hot & Spicy Jerky

1 teaspoon salt
1 ¼ teaspoon black pepper
½ teaspoon cayenne pepper
1 teaspoon onion powder
1 ½ teaspoon paprika
2 garlic cloves (crushed)
2 tablespoons A-1 steak sauce
3 tablespoons Worcestershire sauce

Sweet & Sour Jerky

1 teaspoon salt
1 ¼ teaspoon black pepper
½ teaspoon onion powder
1 garlic clove (crushed)
3 tablespoons brown sugar
1 tablespoon soy sauce
¼ red wine vinegar
¼ cup pineapple juice

Fiesta Jerky

1 teaspoon salt
¼ teaspoon black pepper
1 tablespoon chili powder
1 teaspoon garlic powder
1 teaspoon onion powder
¼ teaspoon ground cumin

Oriental Jerky

1 ½ cup soy sauce
6 drops tabasco sauce
¼ cup white or cane sugar
1 ½ teaspoon ground ginger
¼ teaspoon paprika
1 garlic clove (crushed)

Ragin' Cajun Jerky

1 teaspoon salt
¼ teaspoon black pepper
1 ½ teaspoon coriander
¼ teaspoon chili powder
¼ teaspoon ground ginger
¼ teaspoon turmeric
¼ teaspoon ground cumin

Peppered Teriyaki Jerky

½ teaspoon salt
¼ teaspoon black pepper
½ teaspoon ground ginger
2 teaspoon brown sugar
1 garlic clove (crushed)
1 tablespoon soy sauce

Teriyaki Jerky

1/4 cup soy sauce
1 teaspoon fresh grated ginger root or 1/2 teaspoon ground ginger
2 teaspoons sugar
1 teaspoon salt

Bottle of Soy Jerky

16 oz soy sauce
2 oz liquid smoke
2 oz Worcestershire sauce
2 oz tabasco sauce
1 tablespoon black pepper

Mild Mexican Jerky

1 teaspoon salt
¼ teaspoon black pepper
¼ teaspoon chili powder
½ teaspoon garlic powder
1 teaspoon paprika
1 ½ teaspoon oregano

Granny's Jerky

½ cup soy sauce
2 tablespoons Worcestershire sauce
½ teaspoon onion powder
½ teaspoon garlic powder
¼ teaspoon ginger powder
¼ teaspoon Chinese five-spice powder

Home Style Jerky

¼ cup soy sauce
1 tablespoon Worcestershire sauce
½ teaspoon onion powder
½ teaspoon garlic powder
½ teaspoon black pepper
¾ teaspoon tabasco sauce
½ teaspoon hickory salt

Hawaiian Jerky

1 teaspoon salt
1 teaspoon ground ginger
1 tablespoon brown sugar
¼ teaspoon black pepper
⅛ teaspoon cayenne pepper
1 garlic clove (crushed)
¼ cup pineapple juice
¼ cup soy sauce

EZ Jerky

5 teaspoons salt
5 teaspoons black pepper
1 ½ cup soy sauce
1 cup red wine vinegar
¼ cup brown sugar

Yankee Jerky

5 teaspoons salt
5 teaspoons black pepper
⅓ cup Worcestershire sauce
1 onion, finely chopped

Baja Jerky

5 teaspoons salt
5 teaspoons black pepper
2 tablespoons coriander
1 ½ teaspoons chili powder
1 ½ teaspoons ground ginger
1 ½ teaspoons turmeric
1 ½ teaspoons ground cumin

Oriental Jerky

5 teaspoons salt
5 teaspoons black pepper
1 large onion, minced
5 garlic cloves, pressed
1 cup brown sugar
¼ cup soy sauce
1 ¼ cup red wine
1 ½ cup pineapple juice

Taj Mahal Jerky

5 teaspoons salt
5 teaspoons black pepper
3 teaspoons curry powder
4 garlic cloves, pressed
½ teaspoon cinnamon
3 teaspoon ground ginger
¼ teaspoon ground cloves
1 cup cream sherry

Colorado Jerky

6 teaspoons salt
2 teaspoons black pepper
3 cups beef bouillon

Valley Jerky

1 1/12 cups soy sauce
1 teaspoon nutmeg
5 tablespoons Worcestershire sauce
1 teaspoon ginger
5 teaspoons black pepper
10 teaspoons liquid smoke
4 garlic cloves, crushed
5 teaspoons crushed peppers, dried
1/4 teaspoon onion powder

Jerky Time

1/4 cup soy sauce
3 tablespoons brown sugar
1 tablespoon Hellman's dijonnaise
1 tablespoon Louisiana hot sauce
3 tablespoons ketchup
1 garlic clove, crushed
1 onion, minced
1 tablespoon Worcestershire sauce
2 tablespoons liquid smoke
salt and black pepper to taste

West Coast Jerky

3/4 cup Worcestershire sauce
4 tablespoons liquid smoke
1/2 oz garlic juice
2 garlic cloves, crushed
1/4 teaspoon black pepper
1 teaspoon salt
1/2 cup brown sugar
Louisiana hot sauce to taste (optional)

East Coast Jerky

1 teaspoon salt
1/4 teaspoon black pepper
3 tablespoons brown sugar
1/3 cup red wine vinegar
1/8 teaspoon cayenne pepper
1/3 cup ketchup
1 teaspoon onion powder
1/2 teaspoon garlic powder
1 teaspoon ground mustard

Dixie Jerky

10 oz soy sauce
10 oz teriyaki sauce
1/4 cup Worcestershire sauce
2 tablespoons liquid smoke
1 teaspoon black pepper
1/2 teaspoon cayenne pepper
2 tablespoons brown sugar
1 tablespoon honey
1 tablespoon old bay seasoning

Seven Stuff Jerky

1/2 cup soy sauce
1/2 cup Worcestershire sauce
2 teaspoons accent seasoning
2 teaspoons seasoned salt
2/3 teaspoon garlic powder
2 teaspoons onion powder
2/3 teaspoon black pepper

Hot & Tangy Jerky

1 teaspoon salt
1/4 teaspoon black pepper
1/4 teaspoon cayenne pepper
1 teaspoon onion powder
2 garlic cloves, crushed
2 tablespoons A-1 barbeque sauce
3 tablespoons Worcestershire sauce
1/2 teaspoon paprika

Dale's Cheap Jerky

1 cup liquid smoke
2 cups Worcestershire sauce
4 cups soy sauce
salt and black pepper to taste

Frontier Jerky

1 teaspoon salt
1/4 teaspoon black pepper
2 tablespoons Worcestershire sauce
2 tablespoons liquid smoke
1 teaspoon garlic powder

Damn Good Jerky

3/4 teaspoon salt
1/4 teaspoon black pepper
1 tablespoon brown sugar
2 tablespoons soy sauce
1 tablespoons Worcestershire sauce
1 garlic clove, crushed

New England Jerky

1 teaspoon black pepper
1 teaspoon red pepper
1 teaspoon garlic salt
1 teaspoon hickory salt
10 oz soy sauce
Enough water to cover the whole mess

Old Basic Jerky

1/3 cup liquid smoke
1/3 cup soy sauce
4 tablespoons Worcestershire sauce
1/2 teaspoon black pepper
1/2 teaspoon garlic salt
1 teaspoon accent seasoning

T-Beef Jerky

1/4 cup Worcestershire sauce
1/4 cup soy sauce
1 tablespoon tomato sauce
1 tablespoon vinegar
1 teaspoon white or cane sugar
1/4 teaspoon dried garlic
1/4 teaspoon dried onion
1 teaspoon salt

Well-Seasoned Jerky

1/2 cup soy sauce
1/4 teaspoon garlic powder
1/8 teaspoon black pepper

Peppered Jerky

1/2 teaspoon black pepper (add more for hotter jerky)
1/2 teaspoon garlic powder
1/2 teaspoon onion salt
1/2 cup soy sauce
1/2 teaspoon garlic salt
1/2 teaspoon lemon pepper

Alabama Honey Jerky

1 garlic clove, minced
1/2 cup honey
1 pinch black pepper
1 pinch salt
4 tablespoon lemon juice
1/2 cup soy sauce

Slow & Sweet Jerky

1 cup soy sauce
1 cup water
½ cup molasses
3 garlic cloves, minced
1 tablespoon black pepper
salt to taste

Herb Jerky

1 teaspoon onion salt
1/2 teaspoon salt
1/2 teaspoon garlic salt
1/2 teaspoon lemon pepper
1/2 teaspoon sausage seasoning
1/2 teaspoon thyme
1/2 teaspoon oregano
1/2 teaspoon marjoram
1/2 teaspoon basil

Smoke & Spice Jerky

1/2 cup Worcestershire sauce
1/2 cup soy sauce
1/4 cup brown sugar
4 garlic cloves, crushed
2 teaspoons black pepper
2 teaspoons ground, dried red chili
1 teaspoon onion powder

Thai Beef Jerky

3 tablespoons coriander seeds
1 tablespoons cumin seeds
1 1/2 tablespoon white or cane sugar
4 tablespoons Thai soy sauce
1 1/2 cup oil

Alabama Backwoods Jerky

1/4 teaspoon black pepper
1/4 teaspoon garlic powder
1/2 teaspoon onion powder
1/4 cup soy sauce
1 tablespoon Worcestershire sauce
1 teaspoon liquid smoke

Southern Cured Jerky

1 tablespoon curing salt (For example: Morton's Tender Quick Mix)
1 teaspoon white or cane sugar
1/2 teaspoon black pepper
1/2 teaspoon garlic powder

Onion Beef Jerky

2 oz package of dried onion soup mix
1/4 cup water
1/4 cup soy sauce
1 tablespoon garlic, chopped
1 tablespoon salt

Jesse James Jerky

1 tablespoon Worcestershire sauce
1 tablespoon soy sauce
1/2 tablespoon salt
1/2 tsp ground red pepper
1 cloves sliced garlic
1/2 cup whiskey or bourbon
1/2 cup water

Post Script

We hope you have enjoyed this book as much as we have enjoyed creating it for you. The best part of making jerky is having fun, experimenting and involving the entire family. As you will find, the hardest part of making great jerky is saving some for others!

After making a few batches of jerky with the marinades in this book, try your own recipes. You may have marinade recipes in some obscure corner of your kitchen that would make outstanding jerky. In addition, you could use the marinade recipes in this book for delicious steaks or as marinades for other snacks or meals.

Have fun and indulge in the fine art of jerky makin'.

For more recipes, equipment reviews and information, visit BestJerkyRecipes.com.

Bibliography

Kizer, Ron C. *The Great American Beef Jerky Cookbook*. 1st ed. Vista, California: Little Tiny, 1996. Print.

"History of Jerky." *Jerky.com*. N.p., n.d. Web. 04 Feb. 2014. <http://www.jerky.com/history-of-jerky>.

"History of Jerky." *HiCountry.com*. N.p., n.d. Web. 04 Feb. 2014. <http://www.hicountry.com/from-the-field/history-of-jerky/>.

Printed in Great Britain
by Amazon.co.uk, Ltd.,
Marston Gate.